Doodle Artist

Simply Snowflakes

Annette Rand

www.doodleartist.co.uk

Contents

Copyright © 2015 Annette Rand
All rights reserved

ISBN-13: 978-1517619404

ISBN-10: 1517619408

Printed in Great Britain
by Amazon.co.uk, Ltd.,
Marston Gate.